GW00724774

Bottles with

A play

Mike Tibbetts

Samuel French—London

New York-Toronto-Hollywood

CHARACTERS

Nicola Thompson, *mid-twenties, on the eve of her wedding day*
David Thompson, *Nicola's father*
Sheila Thompson, *Nicola's mother*
Tom Nicholson, *Nicola's prospective husband*

The action takes place in a suburban living-room

The Time —— the present, early on a summer evening

COPYRIGHT INFORMATION
(See also page ii)

This play is fully protected under the Copyright Laws of the British Commonwealth of Nations, the United States of America and all countries of the Berne and Universal Copyright Conventions.

All rights, including Stage, Motion Picture, Radio, Television, Public Reading, and Translation into Foreign Languages, are strictly reserved.

No part of this publication may lawfully be reproduced in ANY form or by any means — photocopying, typescript, recording (including video-recording), manuscript, electronic, mechanical, or otherwise — or be transmitted or stored in a retrieval system, without prior permission.

Licences are issued subject to the understanding that it shall be made clear in all advertising matter that the audience will witness an amateur performance; that the names of the authors of the plays shall be included on all announcements and on all programmes; and that the integrity of the authors' work will be preserved.

The Royalty Fee is subject to contract and subject to variation at the sole discretion of Samuel French Ltd.

In Theatres or Halls seating Four Hundred or more the fee will be subject to negotiation.

In Territories Overseas the fee quoted in this Acting Edition may not apply. A fee will be quoted on application to our local authorized agent, or if there is no such agent, on application to Samuel French Ltd, London.

VIDEO-RECORDING OF AMATEUR PRODUCTIONS

Please note that the copyright laws governing video-recording are extremely complex and that it should not be assumed that any play may be video-recorded for *whatever purpose* without first obtaining the permission of the appropriate agents. The fact that a play is published by Samuel French Ltd does not indicate that video rights are available or that Samuel French Ltd controls such rights.

AUTHOR'S NOTE

It might help directors to know that, while the details of this play are entirely fictitious, the basic situation facing "David" is based on fact. Something like this really happened.

I've described a particular setting and included a lot of stage direction. This is not intended to be followed slavishly, but may be useful in pointing up some of the rhythms and moods in the action.

M. T.

BOTTLES WITH BASKETS ON

A living-room. It is a pleasant summer evening

It could be in any suburban semi in Britain, built any time over the last forty years and furnished in a G-Plan and Dralon sort of way. There is a door to the rest of the house in the back wall; a patio doors to the garden on one side; a "modern" tiled fireplace, with mantelpiece and imitation hearth, on the other side. Over the fireplace is a large framed studio-portrait photograph of a young lady in graduation robes, holding a degree diploma. If we look round the room we see smaller photographs of the same girl at almost every stage of her growing-up

The room is cleared for a function. Furniture has been pushed back to create space in the centre. We see that it's a wedding: a table bears a pile of presents wrapped in unmistakable white and/or silver paper. The mantelpiece bears cards with horseshoes, bells and the tired old gags like plastic ball-and-chain, rolling-pin, etc.

As the Lights come up, David Thompson, mid-forties, is discovered looking out of the patio doors. He is deep in thought. After a while, David moves into the room, slowly looking round, as if trying to remember it all. He fingers some of the wedding presents, reading a gift-tag or two. He ends up in front of the fireplace and looks up at the picture of the girl. He gazes at it in thought for a moment, then leans his hands on the mantelpiece and droops his head forward as if a great weight lay across his shoulders

The door bangs open. Nicola Thompson storms in, seething. She slams the door shut behind her and moves to c. There she relieves herself of a scream which, being constrained behind clenched teeth, amounts to little more than a strangled squeal. With visible effort she begins to calm herself down. She takes a deep breath and makes fiddling little adjustments to her clothing while she struggles to collect herself

We see she is the same girl as in the graduation photo and, since she has much the same hairstyle as in the picture, we may deduce that graduation wasn't all that long ago. Twentyish, pleasant and capable-looking. She's dressed casually for around the house

David's only reaction to her entrance is to lift himself upright again. He still has his back to her

David You OK?

Nicola gives no answer

   (*Turning*) Nicola?

Nicola nods tightly

Nicola I just don't see that my entire wedding is in danger of being ruined because I haven't written out the place cards for the reception yet! (*Pause*) I'm sorry. You'd think I would have got used to Mum by now. But she can still get to me sometimes.

Nicola wants to sit down but has to look round for a seat, since everything is out of place. Eventually she perches on the arm of a settee. She thinks for a moment and then looks up

   How do you stand it, Daddy?
David Stand what?
Nicola Mum. Fussing and — organizing everything. All the time. How could you put up with it all these years?

He seems to struggle momentarily for an answer, but it's light and unconcerned when it comes

David It's not a question of "putting up with it". Your mum just
likes everything to be right that's all. She's — (*with a touch of
weight*) we're both — just trying to do our very best for you.
That's all we've ever wanted.

Nicola (*warmly*) I know.

David (*with a smile*) One thing's for sure. If it hadn't been for your
mother fussing and organizing, there's no way you'd be getting
a proper wedding tomorrow. Left to me, it would be you, Tom and
the Vicar and then a round of drinks at the pub.

Nicola That's not true and you know it. (*She goes to him and puts
her arms around his waist*) You've been wonderful.

David cups his hands tenderly round Nicola's face and studies her

David Has it?

Nicola (*confused by his tone*) Has it what?

David Has it really been wonderful?

Nicola notices that there are tears in her father's eyes

Nicola Daddy, what's the matter?

David I just — suddenly I need very much to be told that I've done
a good job as your father.

Nicola (*with absolute sincerity*) The best.

*Nicola holds his gaze for a moment, then reaches up to brush away
a tear from his cheek. It's almost as if she wants to feel its texture.
David bends forward and kisses her lightly on the tip of her nose. It
seems to be a familiar gesture between them. He turns away from
the embrace. The moment is over*

David I'm sorry. I didn't expect to cry.

Nicola I did. But I didn't expect anyone would see it. (*A brief pause*)
That's something else you're very good at.

David (*turning back to her*) What?

Nicola Not letting people see what you're really feeling.

David But you can read me like a book, eh?
Nicola No. But I've always known that there's a book to read.

Sheila Thompson enters behind them. She holds a notebook to which a pencil is attached by a piece of string. She is Nicola's mother. About the same age as David, she is a bustling, active woman, however, she carries an air of vague anxiety rather than authority

Impassively, Sheila notes the atmosphere between father and daughter

Sheila Calmed down now, have we?
Nicola (*moving to link arms with Sheila*) Well, *I* have. What about you?

Sheila hesitates

David Come on, Sheila, love. Sit down for a minute.
Sheila (*sighing*) There's still a lot to do.
Nicola (*contrite*) I'll finish the place cards tonight. Brownie's honour. (*She holds three fingers up*)

Nicola's mother shakes her head with a half smile

Sheila I just want to get them ticked off, that's all.
Nicola Mum, you're doing a great job of getting everything and everyone completely ticked off.
Sheila (*uncomprehending*) What?

Nicola catches her father's disapproving eye. She pats her mother's arm

Nicola I just mean that you're doing a great job. I appreciate it.

She breaks away from her mother again

Sheila Well, weddings don't arrange themselves, you know. Speaking of which, where's Tom got to? He was supposed to be back here twenty minutes ago.

Nicola You can't pin him down exactly. He wouldn't just pick his mum and dad up from the station and dump them at the hotel. He's got to spend a little time with them.

Sheila We agreed that Mr and Mrs Nicholson would look after their side at the hotel while we got things sorted out here. I'm relying on Tom. There are things I want him to do.

Sheila consults her notebook with a frown

Nicola You know, I still can't believe it.

David What?

Nicola How someone called Nicola Thompson could fall in love with a man named Tom Nicholson. Am I really going to spend the rest of my life as Nicola Nicholson? It sounds like I should have been written by Dickens.

Sheila I don't know. It sort of matches. Anyway, you don't have to change. You could use your maiden name.

Nicola That's no good. It would make him Tom Thompson.

Sheila No, I mean lots of couples nowadays just keep their own names.

Nicola It wouldn't feel like I was properly married. (*She moves away and sits down again*) I want all the traditional bells and whistles. (*She chuckles*) Well, the bells, anyway. And the white dress and confetti and bridesmaids and a three-tier cake — and for people to call me Mrs Thomas Nicholson.

David Not very Women's Lib.

Nicola Don't make fun of me, Daddy.

David Sorry, love. But if it really bothers you, choose a different Christian name.

Sheila Don't be silly, David, her name's Nicola.

David Well, that's what we decided to call her twenty-three years ago. But who says we got it right? I think I've called her "Splodge" more than anything else.

Nicola "Splodge Nicholson" isn't exactly an improvement, Daddy. Of course, if you two had thought to give me a second name, I could have used that. Why didn't you?

Sheila It took us long enough to agree on "Nicola". You know your dad and everything Italian. He was adamant he wanted you to have an Italian-sounding name and that was the only one which seemed at all sensible to me.

Nicola What were the other ones you liked, Daddy?

David (*slightly embarrassed*) Oh, I can't remember.

Sheila Gina was one, I remember.

Nicola Gina Nicholson? Too many "n"'s. (*Trying the accent on for size*) Sophia? Assunta? Concepta?

Sheila Concepta's Irish isn't it?

Nicola Is it? Carla, then. Carla Nicholson. You know, that's not bad.

David There you are, then. Problem solved.

Nicola But I'm not Carla, I'm Nicola.

David Change.

Nicola How? Isn't it a big legal thing?

David I think you just do it if you want to.

This hangs between them for an instant, almost like a challenge

(*In lighter tone*) And the timing's right. You're going to have to tell everybody your new surname and address anyway so you might as well go the whole hog.

Nicola But everybody knows me as Nicola.

David So they'll know you as Carla.

Nicola But you can't suddenly change everything, just like that.

David Why not? (*With sudden emphasis*) Don't ever let change frighten you. If you want to be afraid of something, be afraid of *not* changing. It's taken me a long time to learn that.

Nicola (*struggling to understand*) All right, Daddy.

Sheila (*not really part of this dialogue*) Well, personally I think it's a lot of nonsense, but if Nikki insists on a new name, I think it might be an idea to discuss it with Tom.

Tom Nicholson enters through the patio doors. He carries a plastic supermarket carrier bag. Also in his twenties, he's easy-going and tolerant, but capable when he needs to be

Tom Somebody mention me?

Nicola goes to him and they kiss. David is left, rather abandoned, where he was talking to Nicola

Sheila Are they all safely installed?
Tom Yes.
Sheila (*mentally ticking off her list*) Hotel rooms OK?
Tom Yes, eventually.
Sheila What do you mean, "eventually"?
Tom Shower instead of bath. Don't worry, it's all sorted.
Sheila I knew I should have met them myself.
Tom I said it's sorted. Mum and Dad are perfectly comfortable. Everyone else has arrived safely and the last I saw of them they were all sitting down to a very nice dinner. Dad was passing round old photos of me and Jimmy was asking everyone what they thought Nikki saw in me. I thought the best man was supposed to be on my side. (*Remembering*) Oh, by the way, Mrs Everett wasn't up to the journey.
Sheila (*scribbling*) Ah. That's a shame, but I thought she might not manage it.
Tom She sent a present with Auntie Nola.
Nicola (*to David*) "Nola Nicholson?"
David (*shaking his head*) "N"'s again.
Tom What are you going on about? Auntie Nola's name is Chambers.
Nicola I'll tell you later.
Sheila Tom, would you pop back down to the hotel and give them the final numbers? Mrs Everett was the last question mark.
David Sheila, the lad's staying there tonight. Couldn't he tell them when he goes back later?
Sheila I'd rather he went now, so it's done. I just want to get it ——

Sheila
David } (*in unison*) — ticked off.
Nicola

Tom Don't worry. I don't mind going.

David I'll come with you. We need to get the cars topped up with petrol.(*To Sheila*) Is there anything else, while we're out?

Sheila (*chewing her lip*) Not that I can think of on the spur. I'll phone and catch you at the hotel if I think of anything.

David Right. (*He raises his eyebrows at Tom*)

Tom Oh, by the way. This is for you from my dad. (*He holds out the carrier bag*)

David opens the bag and takes out a distinctive bottle covered in raffia

I hope you like Chianti. I've no idea if it's any good. I only know it's Chianti from the basket on the bottle.

David looks at the bottle and shakes his head, smiling at some inner joke. It must be a good one, because he chuckles and then starts to laugh heartily. He sets the bottle down somewhere

Then, still laughing, David exits through the patio doors

Tom watches David with amusement, shrugs his shoulders to Sheila and Nicola and exits after David

Nicola moves to shut the patio doors after the men. She rubs her arm. The evening is turning chilly

Nicola I think the strain is beginning to tell on Dad.

Her mother makes no comment

(*Nicola glances at Sheila,then looks back outside*) I hope the weather stays like today.

Sheila The forecast at six o'clock said — (*she consults a page in her notebook*) — "possible showers with an anticyclone approaching from the West later in the day".

Nicola What does that add up to?

Sheila I think it means they don't really know.

Nicola moves to sit again

Nicola What was it like for you and Dad?

Sheila What was what like?

Nicola When you got married. What was the weather like?

Sheila (*remembering fondly*) Oh, it was a lovely day. We had the last of the daffodils and the first of the tulips. Typical April.

Mention of the month sparks a thought in Nicola's mind

Nicola Mum, if I asked you a question would you give me an honest answer?

Sheila What about?

Nicola Me.

Sheila Go on, then.

Nicola Was I really born prematurely?

Sheila (*uncomfortable*) You know you were. What sort of a question's that?

Nicola I'd like to know the truth. Did you and Dad make love before you were married?

Sheila I'm not sure this is the sort of thing I should be discussing with you.

Nicola Oh, come on. Tomorrow I'll be an old married woman like you. I mean, it was the swinging seventies. Flower power and free love and all that. Did you?

Sheila Your Dad and I weren't exactly hippies. (*She pauses, then, with finality*) You were a honeymoon baby, born at twenty minutes past noon on the fourth of December, six and a half weeks premature.

Nicola thinks about this for a moment

Nicola I used to imagine that I was a love-child, conceived in wild passion and born out of wedlock, the product of an uncontrollable love! Mills and Boon eat your heart out.

Sheila I'm sorry to spoil your fantasy, but it was all very ordinary and respectable.

Nicola What was Dad like, then?

Sheila He was very nice.

Nicola Nice! Is that all?

Sheila What's wrong with nice?

Nicola Where did you meet?

Sheila I must have told you all this.

Nicola No, you never talk about it. Tell me now. What was the first time your eyes met his?

Sheila (*remembering fondly*) It was at a party. He was sitting on the floor in a circle of people, playing his guitar and singing. I asked him if he knew something-or-other and he sang it all the way through for me. Even better than the record.

Nicola A guitar? Dad?

Sheila Oh yes. In those days.

Nicola So he sang to you. Romantic old thing. Then what?

Sheila Well, he asked me out. Pictures, dancing, Chinese restaurants and so on. We got on very well together, so it became a regular thing.

Nicola How soon did you get married?

Sheila Not for a long while. Nearly three years.

Nicola Why so long?

Sheila We didn't feel there was any hurry. We enjoyed each other's company and that was all we needed at the time.

Nicola So what happened? Did he just propose to you one day, or what?

Sheila Look, this is ridiculous! I've got a thousand and one things I should be doing ...

Nicola (*stopping her*) No. Please, Mum, go on. I'm really interested. When did he ask you to marry him?

Sheila (*returning to her memories*) Oh, your poor dad. He went out and booked this big holiday in Italy. Three weeks travelling all over. I think he was expecting me to go with him, but I didn't fancy it. You know I'm not a globetrotter. Anyway, he covered up by saying he really wanted to go on his own. It was only after he'd gone I wondered if he was planning to pop the question in Florence or some romantic place like that. Maybe I'd spoiled all his plans. I felt awful. I remember I wrote him this letter telling him how sorry I was. But it was all right. When he came back, we just booked the Registry Office and got on with it. Then you came along and here we are.

There's a pause while they think of the next thing to say

Nicola Have you been happy, Mum?

Sheila Yes, love, of course.

Nicola No, seriously. Have things worked out the way you wanted them to?

Sheila Well, life — I mean — you have to take the rough with the smooth. It's never all plain sailing. (*With emphasis*) But the thing I've always had is the knowledge that your dad loves me. Really loves me. Every day he does something which shows me how much. (*Self-assured*) That's the way it's been, ever since the beginning, and it always will. (*She smiles tightly, almost sadly, at Nicola*) If you and Tom can say the same in twenty years' time, you'll be doing well.

Nicola thinks about this

Nicola I never knew Dad could play the guitar.

Sheila He's still got it somewhere I think. You know what he's like. He never throws anything away.

Nicola Where would he have it?

Sheila In the loft, I suppose.

Nicola I wonder why he's never played it all these years?

Sheila I don't suppose he's had much time for that sort of thing.

Nicola Well he's going to have time for it now, isn't he? I mean, it'll just be the two of you again after tomorrow. Listen, why don't we get him to play it again? After all, this is a sort of last night together, isn't it?

Sheila I'm sure your Dad will have forgotten it all long ago.

Nicola I bet he hasn't. I'm going to see if I can find it anyway.

Nicola dashes out

Sheila goes to the door, as if to call after Nicola, but she doesn't. Instead, she turns back and glances worriedly round the room. Her eyes fix on something and she nods emphatically

Sheila Bowls for the peanuts.

Sheila goes out, making another note in her book

There is a pause

Tom and David enter through the patio doors

David Anyway, I got really fed up with this. I mean, we're killing ourselves to pay for this fancy prep school. So one day I pick her up in the car and I ask her the same question, "What did you do today?" And I get the same old answer, "Nothing". So I lost my rag. I said to her, "Nicola, you've spent five hours in classes where a lot of people have tried to teach you things and you come home and tell me you remember nothing about it. It's not good enough. Now I'll ask you again, what did you learn about today?" "I've told you, Daddy," she says, getting all tearful, "We learned about nothing. The number nothing. It's a big round circle like an 'O'!"

Tom laughs politely

Tom She's learned a lot since then.

David Yes, she's done well. Mind you she's worked hard to get a good career. You both have.

Tom We'll need to watch that. I mean, we've been really lucky to get jobs together in Southampton, but sooner or later moves are on the cards for both of us. I suppose it's a toss-up whether I'll have to move to follow Nik or vice versa.

David Is that likely to be a problem?

Tom Not while there's just the two of us, but it's not clear where children might fit in.

David In my experience, children tend to fit themselves in, convenient or not.

Sheila enters

Sheila Oh good, Tom, you're back. I need those cases of wine brought in from the garage. Can I borrow you for a minute?

Tom OK. I'm still a free man until eleven o'clock tomorrow.

Sheila (*frowning*) That's not how you see it, is it, Tom?

Tom What?

Sheila Giving up your freedom. Marriage, I mean.

Tom No, of course not. It's just the way people talk about weddings. I'm sorry. I suppose it's just a funny time — I'll get the wine. (*He starts to exit, then pauses*) You do know how much I love Nikki? I mean — it'll be all right.

Tom exits

Sheila (*looking off after Tom*) Will they be all right, d'you suppose?

David Oh, I think so.

Sheila You can't tell these days, though, can you?

David It's really up to them.

Sheila I suppose so. You can't live someone else's life for them, can you?

David Can't you?

Sheila turns to him

Sheila That's a strange thing to say.

David Well, isn't that what marriage is? Living for someone else rather than just for yourself?

Sheila You make it sound like a terrible sacrifice.

David Not terrible, but it *is* a sacrifice. I mean, you could have done a lot more if you hadn't been saddled with a family.

Sheila Me?

David Yes.

Sheila What could I have done?

David That's the point. You never even ask the question. Don't you wonder about the possibilities? What might still be possible?

Sheila What's wrong with being a housewife and mother?

David Nothing at all. It's just not the be-all and end-all. You're worth more than a lifetime of washing-up and ironing.

Sheila Tom's right. It is a funny time. (*A change of mood*) I'm so glad they're getting married in church.

David Because we had a Registry Office quickie?

Sheila Partly. But the church service makes it much more — formal. I really want them to understand those vows tomorrow.

A pause

David (*delicately*) Sheila. When we made our vows to each other, did we understand them?

Sheila Oh yes, I think so.

David All of them?

Sheila frowns at David

Tom puts his head round the door

Tom That's the wine in. I'm not sure I've stacked it where you want it, though.

Sheila (*breaking away from David*) Let me have a look ...

Sheila bustles out again. With a rueful grin at David, Tom follows her out

David wanders around the room, rather aimlessly, until he spots the bottle of Chianti where he left it. He opens a bureau drawer (unlike much of the furniture it hasn't been moved, so he knows exactly where it is)——and takes out a corkscrew. He opens the bottle. But he can't find a glass. He looks in a cupboard and around the room. He pauses and then takes a small flower vase off the mantelpiece. He throws the posy and its water out of the patio door and wipes the vase with the corner of a table cloth. He pours himself some wine and tastes it. He holds up the bottle to examine it

David (*in an inexplicable broad "North Country" accent*) A bottle with a basket on!

Nicola comes in. She seems tense

David You're welcome to some of this, but you'll have to find your own vase.

Nicola doesn't answer

What's up?

Nicola looks at him for a moment. Then she turns away

Nicola (*apparently lightly*) Is it any good?
David What?
Nicola Tom's dad's wine.
David It's not bad.
Nicola You prefer Chianti Classico. You've always drunk that.
David When we could afford it.
Nicola I used to have a little tin full of the labels off the necks of the bottles. You once showed me how you could tell real Chianti Classico by the little picture of a black cockerel. After that I soaked every one off the bottle and kept it.
David Why?
Nicola I suppose it was my way of sharing something quite personal with you. It was almost like a secret between us.

David I never knew.

Nicola (*levelly*) There's probably lots of things we never knew about each other. (*Lighter*) I was asking Mummy some questions before — about the old days.

David (*frowning*) Oh yes?

Nicola She told me that you used to play the guitar at parties. She said that was how you met. You sang a song to her.

David (*controlled*) That's right.

Nicola I never knew you were so romantic.

There's a growing tension between them. They feel for the next step

David It wasn't all that romantic. (*He attempts a disarming grin*) You haven't heard me play the guitar!

Nicola Why?

David Why what?

Nicola Why haven't I ever heard you play your guitar for us?

David There — never seemed to be the right opportunity.

Nicola Mum said you still had the guitar in the loft. (*She takes the plunge*) I went to look for it.

David (*looking down into his glass*) And you found it?

Nicola I found a guitar case. There was a guitar in it, but there were a lot of other things, too.

David Like what?

Nicola Like these. (*She produces a small sheaf of documents and tosses them on to a table*) Letters from an Italian estate agent, statements from an Italian bank account, loads of cancelled cheques paid to a Signora Castelvecchi — (*bitterly*) — *Nicola* Castelvecchi.

David (*still not looking at her*) And — what do you make of all that?

Nicola How long has this long-range affair been going on, Daddy?

A long moment. David puts down his vase and walks to look out of the patio doors

David Where did I go wrong?

Nicola What?

David When did I give myself away?

Nicola What are you talking about? It's obvious! You own a house in Tuscany that none of us know about. You've got a secret bank account in Florence and you've been paying money to some Italian woman we've never heard of!

David It must have been earlier, maybe years ago. I slipped up somewhere along the line; gave something away. (*He turns to face her*) You must have thought all along that I was capable of something like this, to be so ready to believe the worst.

Nicola is nonplussed. David speaks insistently, almost aggressively, like an interrogator

David Was I away too much? Was that it?

Nicola What?

David All those nights I spent away from home. You cried yourself to sleep wishing that Daddy could be there to kiss you good-night?

Nicola No — you were never away ——

David The tension at home, then? Between me and Mummy. The arguments and fights?

Nicola There weren't any. You never argued.

David What was it, then? Didn't I give you enough presents? Didn't I make you feel I was thinking about you every minute of every day? (*Driving this home*) Didn't I *love* you enough?

Nicola Yes — (*a little girl's whimper*) Daddy!

They break off. David turns back to look into the garden. Nicola collects her thoughts

Are you saying you're *not* having an affair?

David (*flatly*) Signora Castelvecchi is sixty-five, if she's a day. She has three grown-up daughters, two sons and, at the last count, five grandchildren. She supplements her husband's small pension by working as a housekeeper for foreigners who buy property in her village.

Father and daughter study each other, each trying to gauge the other's thoughts

Nicola (*softer*) Daddy. What's going on?

David seems about to tell her. Then he visibly shies away from it. He breaks away from her

David Oh, Nikki. Look, we've all got enough on our plate tonight. Couldn't you wait until after tomorrow? It'll all become clear then.

Nicola Dad, please tell me now. However bad it is, it can't spoil tomorrow more than imagining and worrying about it.

David rubs his eyes with his hands

David I should have known. I should have put my foot down with your mum and just booked dinner with the Nicholsons tonight. (*He shakes his head*) To get so close. One day! (*He takes a deep breath*) I didn't want it this way. The idea was that you and Tom would have a fabulous wedding day, go off on honeymoon and not find out anything till you got back.

Nicola Find out about what? For God's sake, Dad ...

David I am not having an affair with anyone. I've always been faithful to your Mum. But I *am* leaving her. Not for another woman. Just to be on my own.

Nicola (*struggling to take in the implications of this*) Leaving — when?

David Tomorrow night. It was to be right after everyone had gone.

Nicola But what about Mum? How could you do this to her?

David Your mother knows all about it.

Nicola What?

David She agreed to it.

Nicola But — a minute ago, she was telling me how much you loved her ... !

David I *have* loved her. But I've never been in love with her.

Nicola (*anger and tears starting*) That's *bullshit!* She told me the
whole thing. How you planned to propose to her on holiday, and
she felt bad about spoiling it and you came home and married her
anyway, and — (*she becomes helpless*) — you must have loved
her, Daddy, because you had *me!*

David takes hold of Nicola and draws her to him

David That's absolutely right, Nikki. I loved her because we had
you.

*Nicola takes this in. When David sees she has heard, he releases her
again*

What your mum told you was pretty much the truth, but she
missed out some important bits. Do you want to hear the whole
story?

Nicola nods

We met at a party, just like you said. We went out together for two
years or more, and I mean just that. We went out. Cinema, parties,
meals out. We just did social things together. We were both living
at home with our parents, so apart from a kiss good-night, there
was never anything physical. But it wasn't just that we had no
opportunity. I enjoyed being with your mum. She was good fun,
but I never felt — passionate about her.

Nicola Weren't you interested in sex?

David (*disconcerted by her directness*) As much as anyone, I
suppose. But I always thought that would come along later. With
somebody else. You see, I thought of your mum as a good friend,
but I never really saw it as a permanent thing.

Nicola But she did?

David Time goes by so fast. Over two years we came to be thought
of as a couple. It was always "David and Sheila". Our families
knew each other. Everyone just assumed we would get married
sooner or later. Then I realized that Sheila thought so too.

Nicola Why didn't you tell her how you felt?

David I tried to. For six months. But I was a real coward about hurting her. Two years is a long time. Even though I'd said nothing definite, it seemed to me that Sheila was entitled to feel we were — attached.

Nicola So what happened?

David I got my job at the factory. My first decent salary. On the strength of it I decided to move away from home into my own flat. More of a bedsit, really. I could only afford to rent. Sheila helped me to move in. At the end of the day we were sitting on the bed with a Chinese take-away and a bottle of plonk. I didn't even have a table. We finished the food — and the bottle ——

Nicola —and nature took its course.

David It was almost as if we were alone for the first time. As if the possibility of — doing anything — had never arisen before. I can remember thinking that I wasn't sure I wanted this to happen, but it seemed too late to say no. (*Pause*) It was the first time for both of us. (*He breaks off*) Nikki, I'm sorry. This is no way for a father to talk to his daughter.

Nicola Dad, we have to. Keep going.

David retrieves his little vase and pours himself more wine

David Are you sure you won't have some of this?

She shakes her head. He goes on with his story

I don't know what you're supposed to feel after your first time, but I felt awful. It finally brought home to me that Sheila and I weren't right for each other. But now I was in deeper than ever. I decided I had to call a halt. I wasn't starting the new job for a couple of months, but I made some excuses about work to avoid her for a week or two. Then I arranged to meet her. It was in a park. I just told her everything.

Nicola What did she say?

David Nothing. She just sat there, absolutely still. I remember wishing she'd do something. Have hysterics even. But she didn't even look at me. In the end I just walked away. I told her not to try and contact me because I was going away for a while.

Nicola The holiday in Italy.

David I actually made that up on the spot to stop her getting in touch again. But afterwards it seemed like a good idea, so I went to a travel agent. I booked the first thing I saw — a charter flight to Rome.

Nicola This whole thing with Italy. Is that when it started?

David You have to understand what I was like then, Nikki. I was young and I'd lived at home all my life. I'd never been anywhere or done anything.

Nicola Mum said she thought you were nice.

David Imagine the sort of man your mum would call "nice".

Nicola Even my Tom only managed "nice enough".

David There you are then. (*He shakes his head, remembering*) I was on the plane before I realized what I had done. All I had was a return air ticket three weeks later. No hotels, no package or anything. I'd never so much as been Youth Hostelling before! I couldn't even speak Italian. I honestly wondered how I was going to survive.

Nicola How did you?

David One step at a time. I cadged a lift with the bus that was taking all the package tourists into the city. They dropped us at this hotel somewhere near St. Peter's. The hotel was all right but the area looked awful. A narrow street jammed with motor scooters and clapped-out little cars. Men drinking in bars like dark caves in the whitewashed buildings. They all looked like they carried knives. (*Pause*) The hotel handed out packs to everyone else in the group. They all got room keys, meal vouchers and itineraries for trips and things. It seemed so safe and easy for them. I tried to get a room for myself but they were full. I booked myself a room for the last night of my trip, so that I could get the bus back to the airport. So — there I was, on the street with my little knapsack.

Nicola How did you get on?

David I can still hardly believe it, Nikki. Rome, Florence, Siena.

Churches that make ours look like garages. Art. Music. I found the world's cheapest rum and coke in a Communist Party headquarters. I ate a two foot pizza one night, but got so drunk that I was never able to find the restaurant again. Sitting on a gargoyle in a church listening to Vivaldi. The owner of a backstreet restaurant, making up poetry on slates while he cooked the food. Or the guy with the coffee bar in Florence. He couldn't afford ever to close, but his wife brought his kid to say good-night at eleven o'clock every night. (*He holds up his vase, still with a little wine in it*) I spent the last two weeks in Tuscany. Chianti Classico country, the *Gallo Nero*. (*He smiles at her*) The Black Cock. Cobbled roads through miles of vineyards. Little farm restaurants where the first bottle appears in seconds but it takes two hours to get any food. But the wine slides down as smoothly as time slips away. (*He drains his vase and goes to refill it*)

Nicola As smoothly as that stuff is sliding down?

David (*looking at the bottle and snorting*) This? (*He shakes his head*) One night I walked to the restaurant run by a small winery near where I was staying. They were having a sort of barbecue on the terrace at the back. It was a private function but they welcomed me in all the same. Somebody started to sing and by chance I knew the tune. I saw a guitar in the corner, so I picked it up and played along. It was after midnight when they let me stop. They liked Beatles numbers best. (*Almost under his breath*) "We all-a leeve inna yaylo sahmarine, yaylo sahmarine ..." I went back every night and played for my supper. And every night I got a different bottle of Chianti. The best *riservas*. From Radda and Castellina — vinsantos made from raisins — (*He pauses*) The night before I drove back to Rome the patron offered me a job. He would teach me to cook, I would teach him the guitar. I said I'd think about it. (*A brief pause*) When I got back to the hotel in Rome I met one of the men who'd been on the package holiday. (*He affects the broad North-Country accent we heard earlier*) "We had a wine-tasting," he says. They'd told me about these in Chianti. Traders looking to unload some cheap wine. But always bottled in flasks covered with straw to look like the good stuff and catch the tourist trade. "Did you get any to take home?" he asked me. I showed him the Patron's goodbye present. An Antinori you'd pay forty quid for in London. "Oh," says this bloke, "an ordinary 'un. You should have stuck with us, lad. We got bottles wi' baskets on!" Suddenly I saw that all my life I'd been accepting the safe, obvious options. I'd just gone along with other people and put up with second-rate "bottles wi' baskets on" because it seemed too risky to reach for anything better. I think that was the moment I decided to accept the Patron's offer and pack up in Britain.

Nicola But you didn't. Why not?

David (*becoming matter-of-fact*) When I checked in for the flight there was a letter waiting for me. It had been forwarded by the airline. It was from your mum. She told me that she was pregnant.

Nicola Me?

David nods

David I went to see her as soon as I got back. She was in a dreadful state. (*He goes to look at the picture over the fireplace*) I made a deal with her. I would come back to her and I would marry her. We would live together and we would bring up the child. I would do everything in my power to give her and the baby a normal family life, including all the love and care I had in me. But there was a clear condition. As soon as the baby grew up and left home, I would leave too and get on with whatever life was left to me.

Nicola And Mum agreed to this?

David Oh yes. It was clearly understood.

Nicola That's quite a story, Dad.

David I'm sorry you had to learn the truth like this.

Nicola If it is the truth.

David turns to look at Nicola. She holds his stare for a moment and then goes to the interior door

(*Opening the door and calling*) Mum! Mum!

Tom appears

Tom What's up?
Nicola (*ignoring him*) Mum!

Sheila appears, licking the flap of an envelope

Sheila Make it quick, will you dear? I've got a mountain of these
thank you letters to finish.
Nicola (*wrong-footed for an instant*) Thank you for what?
Sheila For your wedding presents.
Nicola But we haven't unwrapped them yet. We don't know what
anyone sent.
Sheila Yes we do. Underwood's told me today what everybody had
bought from our list.
Nicola (*after a hesitation to digest this logic*) Dad says he's leaving
you.

Sheila freezes, the envelope flap still in contact with her tongue

He says you know all about it. That you agreed to it.
Sheila (*turning to look at her husband, the envelope fluttering from
her fingers*) David?
David I told her the truth, Sheila.
Tom Truth? What about? What on earth's been going on ... ?
Nicola (*silencing him*) About me. How I was born. How they got
married.
Sheila (*to Nicola*) But — I — told you how we ... (*back to David*)
David, what have you been saying?
David Nicola found my guitar case. It had — things in it. Things
I didn't intend to come out until after tomorrow. I had to tell her
the whole story. What we agreed, right from the very beginning.
Sheila What story? What things in the guitar case? (*with rising
panic*) David, stop this. You're frightening me.

*Sheila staggers backwards a step. Tom steps quickly forward and
pulls out a chair for her. She sits down*

David Sheila, please. This is as difficult for me as it is for you. Don't make it any harder.

Sheila stares at him, almost in horror. Nicola kneels beside her mother

Nicola Dad says he never wanted to marry you. He says he only came back to you because you wrote to him in Italy telling him you were having me. He says you both agreed that he would leave after I grew up. He says you've known all along that this was going to happen. (*She pauses, anguished*) Mummy, is that true?

Sheila has tears in her eyes, but steel in her voice

Sheila I don't know what you're talking about! (*She stands up. Intermittent sobs cannot undermine the solid gravity of what she says*) I — have heard of — mid-life crisis or nervous breakdowns, but I never thought they could make a person — invent — such a — sick — cruel — lie!

David (*hanging his head, closing his eyes, as if in pain*) It isn't a lie, Sheila. You know it isn't ...

Sheila (*angry now*) No. I don't know! I don't know why you're doing this! I don't know what's got into your head. A minute ago I would have told anybody who asked that you were the perfect husband. Now I don't even know who you are!

David You've always known ...

Sheila I've always known you've had a strange obsession with Italy! But I thought it was harmless dreaming!

David (*almost pleading*) Sheila, listen ...

Sheila No, you listen! Tomorrow is my daughter's wedding day. The happiest day of her life. And mine. I've looked forward to it for years and nobody, not you, not your sick fantasies, are going to spoil it. (*She pauses, forcing down the lid on her emotions*) We're going to stop talking about it now. Let's just think about the wedding. And then, after tomorrow, we'll sort things out. (*She looks at David*) All right, David?

He doesn't reply

Right. (*She retrieves the envelope she brought in and carefully sticks down the flap. She smoothes the letter between her hands and looks at the others, almost defiantly*) Right.

Sheila sits back down by Nicola and, a moment later, crumbles silently into convulsive tears. Tom moves to stand behind her, his hands on her shoulders. Tom looks balefully at David

Tom I don't know about the rest of it, but your timing's bloody awful, David.
David Nikki?

Nicola stands up and retrieves the bottle of Chianti. She hands it disinterestedly to David

Nicola Just finish your wine, Daddy.

David grabs Nicola's wrist. The bottle in her fist is suspended between them

David You believe me, don't you?
Nicola What do you expect? A few minutes ago you were just my dad. Safe and dependable. Now you're trying to tell me that everything I've ever known is — make-believe! All my life I've known you as one thing. How on earth do you expect me — on an instant — to start thinking of you as something else?
David I think you just do it. If you want to.
Nicola (*close to tears*) I just want my daddy back!

Nicola thrusts the bottle against David's chest. David takes it from her, then stands with the hand holding the bottle dangling at his side. There is a tired hiatus in the action. Nicola goes back to her mum. David regards the embracing group

David Sheila, I need you to help me.

Sheila Help you? To throw away our entire lives? Destroy
everything we've worked for?

David (*realizing*) You really think that, don't you? You've just —
put it all out of your mind.

*David turns away from them. The weight of the bottle seems to be
dragging him down*

Sheila This is a mess.

Tom You could say that.

Sheila No, I mean in here. Nobody else seems to care, but we have
a houseful of guests tomorrow. I was ready for them. Now look
at the place.

Tom Don't worry. I'll clear it up.

*Tom straightens up some furniture and then goes to David's
documents. He is gathering them together when he spots something.
He picks up a used envelope and reads the address. Without a word,
he taps Nicola on the shoulder and hands it to her. She studies the
address. Then she looks up*

Nicola Daddy?

David makes no response

What's this?

David turns, and sees what she's holding

David Don't, Nikki. (*He glances at Sheila*) I hadn't realized — this
is more complicated than I thought. Just — put it down.

Nicola I have to know, Daddy

Tom God! Haven't you had enough for one night ...?

Nicola (*cutting him off*) Shut up, Tom!

Nicola opens the envelope and unfolds a sheet of writing paper

(*reading*) "Dear David. I know you said you wanted nothing more to do with me and that I was not to try and track you down, but I hope you will understand when I tell you ..." (*She trails away*)

David (*taking up the reading from memory*) "... when I tell you that I am pregnant. There is no doubt about it. I have been to the doctor. My family must not know. I have nobody else to turn to. It is your baby as well. You must come back and help me. Even though you don't love me any more, you owe it to our child."

Nicola takes the letter to her mum and holds it out to her. Sheila does not take it, but stares at it blankly

Nicola Mum, is it true?

Sheila (*long hesitation. Then, something tearing inside her*) I — don't want it to be true ...

Nicola Is it?

David Sheila, you don't have to ...

Sheila I — never thought he really meant it. (*She looks up at Nicola and Tom, almost hunted*) In all this time, he's never mentioned it again. Twenty-three years. Not once.

David (*going to her*) That was the deal. I promised you a normal family life. I said I would do my best for you. My best. Never second-best. That meant burying it completely, for however long, to let you forget. To let you be happy. But I never forgot. Not for a single day. (*Urgently*) You *have* been happy, haven't you, Sheila?

Sheila Oh, David. (*She nods*) You've always done your best. You've loved and cared for us. I've been very happy. But haven't you? We've loved and cared for you as well.

David (*torn*) Yes ...

Sheila Well, then?

David (*through gritted teeth*) We agreed. It was understood ...

Sheila Why? What are you going *for*, David? You've got a good life here. What is there for you in Italy?

David I —— don't know. That's what I want to find out.

Sheila My poor love. (*Tenderly, she puts a hand to smooth David's face*) It was a dream, David. A castle in the air we built when we were very young, to get us over a bad time. But we're not twenty any more. (*She speaks as if comforting a child*) Over the years we've built something real. That has to count for something. Even if it hasn't been everything you wanted for yourself, it's been enough, hasn't it? You're safe here. You've got us to look after you. And in spite of everything, we still need you to look after us. (*She kisses him softly. Their foreheads rest together*) The wine we made together may not be the very best quality, but twenty-three years isn't so bad a vintage.

Nicola (*sharply*) Daddy, go now! (*She pulls her father to his feet*) Tonight. Don't wait until tomorrow. Don't bother to pack, just throw a few things in a rucksack!

David (*confused*) But ... (*he indicates Sheila*)

Nicola No. Don't think about us. Just go.

Tom Nik, I really think if David wants to stay ...

Nicola He *doesn't!* Don't you see? It's happening to him all over again! (*She scrabbles together the documents and thrusts them before David's eyes*) I can't imagine what it's going to be like not to have you and Mum together, but we'll tackle it. One step at a time. You told me tonight to be more afraid of *not* changing! (*She grabs his chin to focus his eyes on hers. She speaks quietly but intently to him*) You gave me everything, Dad. You gave me my life and you've given me twenty-three years of yours. I won't let you give any more.

Nicola stuffs the documents into one of David's pockets

Sheila But — tomorrow. If your Dad ... who's going to give you away?

Nicola *I'll* give me away! And I'm giving my Dad away tonight.

David still hesitates

Oh, Dad, don't give up. Don't stop searching for something better. Do it for me. (*She cracks and hammers a fist on his chest*) Dammit, for once in your life, before it's too late, do it for *you!*

David backs away to the interior door. He turns to grasp the handle

Daddy ...

David turns back to the room. She moves to him

You won't need that.

She reaches down and takes the Chianti bottle from his hand. He kisses her on the tip of her nose. She flings her arms round his neck, then breaks free and pushes him to the door. She smiles through tears

No more bottles with baskets on.

David turns to exit through the door, then looks back at them all

Black-out

CURTAIN

FURNITURE AND PROPERTY LIST

On stage: Mantelpiece. *On it:* wedding cards, horseshoes, wedding bells, plastic ball-and-chain, rolling pin, small vase with posy. *Over it:* **Nicola**'s graduation portrait
Settee
Chairs
Bureau. *In it:* corkscrew
Cupboard
Table. *On it:* table-cloth, wedding presents wrapped in white/silver paper with tags
Photographs of **Nicola**

Off stage: Notebook with pencil attached (**Sheila**)
Carrier bag. *In it:* raffia-covered bottle of Chianti (**Tom**)
Letters, statements, cheques (**Nicola**)
Envelope (**Sheila**)

LIGHTING PLOT

To open: Overall general lighting

Cue 1   **David** turns back to look at them all   (Page 30)
          Black-out

EFFECTS PLOT

No cues